Looking After My Balls

Sheila Hollins and Justin Wilson
illustrated by Beth Webb

Books Beyond Words
RCPsych Publications/St George's, University of London
LONDON

First edition 2004, Gaskell/St George's Hospital Medical School.

Reprinted with amendments 2009, RCPsych Publications/St George's, University of London.

Text and illustrations © Sheila Hollins & Beth Webb 2004, 2009.

ISBN 978-1-904671-05-3

British Library Cataloguing-in-Publication Data

A catalogue record for this book is available from the British Library.

Distributed in North America by Publishers Storage and Shipping Company.

Printed and bound by ArtQuarters Press Limited, London.

The Royal College of Psychiatrists is a charity registered in England and Wales (228636) and in Scotland (SC038369). St George's Hospital Charity is a registered charity (no. 241527).

Further information about the Books Beyond Words series can be obtained from: Royal College of Psychiatrists, 17 Belgrave Square, London SW1X 8PG (tel: 020 7235 2351; fax 020 7245 1231; website www.rcpsych.ac.uk/bbw).

Authors

Sheila Hollins is Professor of Psychiatry of Learning Disability at St George's Hospital Medical School, University of London; Justin Wilson, Consultant in Psychiatry of Learning Disability, is involved in research at St George's Hospital Medical School. Beth Webb has pioneered the use of emotional colour and mime in her illustrations for the Books Beyond Words series.

Acknowledgements

We would like to thank our editorial advisors Paul Adeline and Gary Butler, and the Men's Groups at the Crescent Resource Centre and the Joan Bicknell Centre, for helping us to think of ideas for this book and for telling us what was needed in the pictures. Our thanks to the clients at the Cranstock day service who also told us what was needed in the pictures.

We were very lucky to have representatives on the book's Advisory Group from CancerBACUP, Cancer Research UK, the Department of Health, Kingston CTPLD, the Orchid Trust, St George's Hospital Medical School, and West Middlesex University Hospital: Joan Austoker, Danny Bungaroo, Debbie Coates, Tim Elliott, Abbas Khadra, Colin Osborne, Hugh Rogers and Gill Rowland.

Our thanks to the nurse specialists at CancerBACUP who gave us such useful feedback.

Finally, we would like to thank the Department of Health for providing financial support for the project.

3

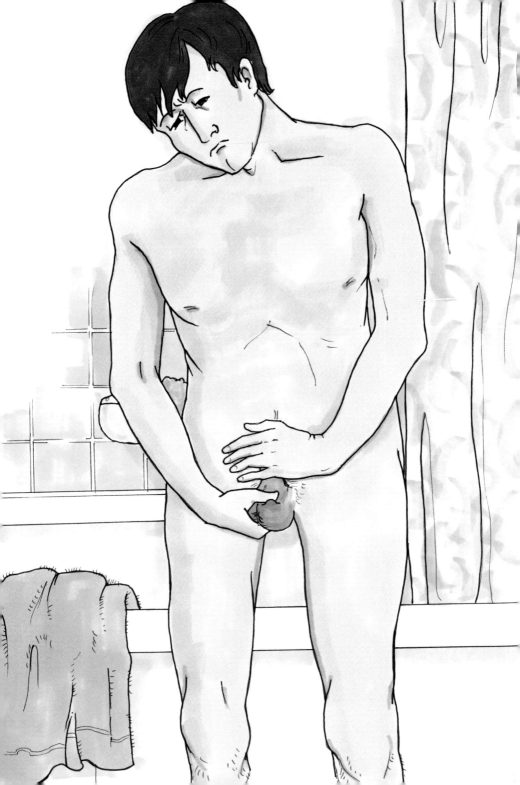

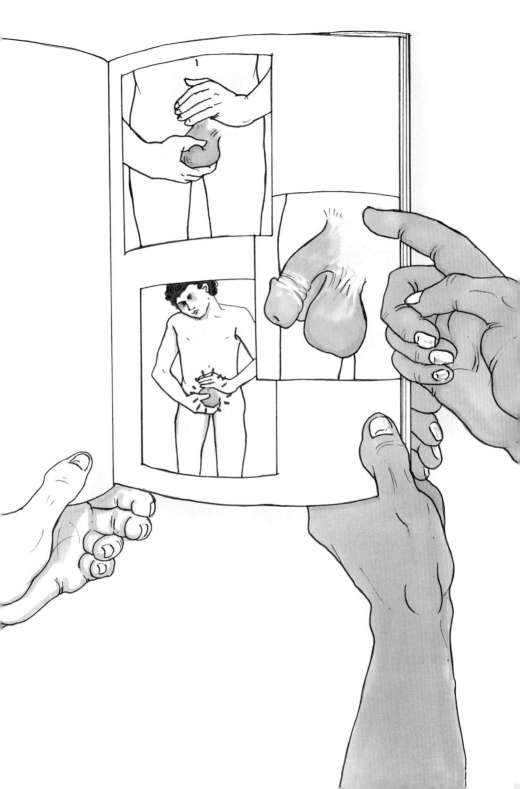

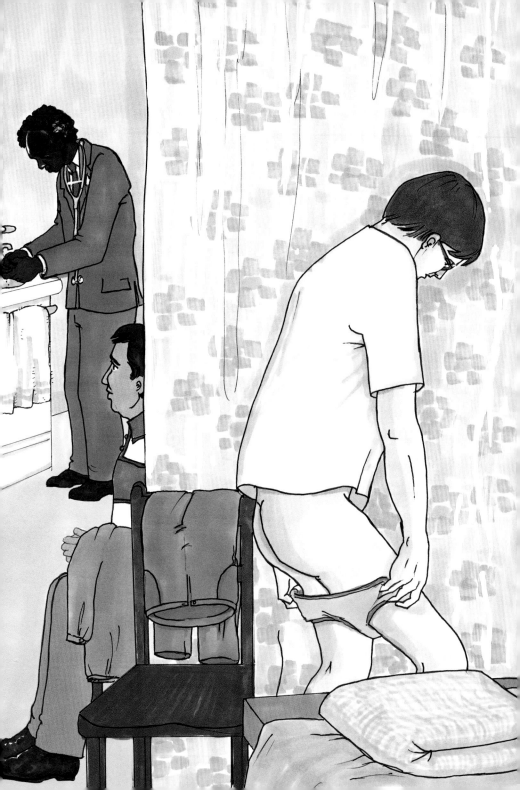

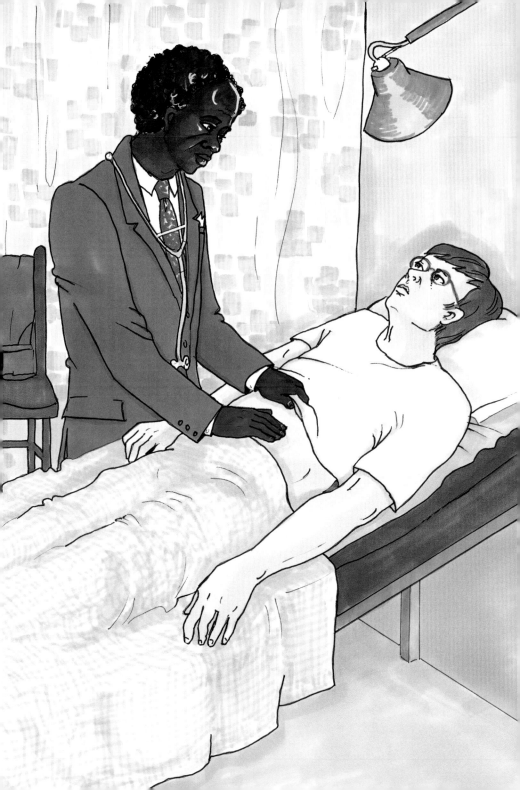

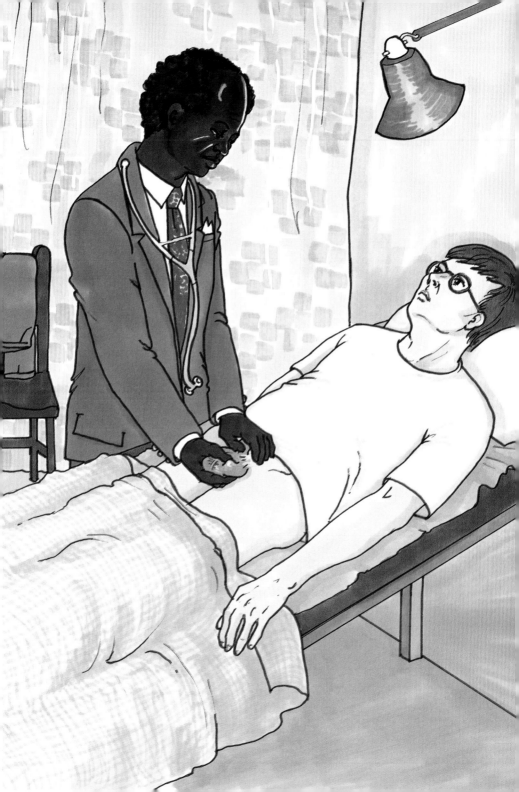

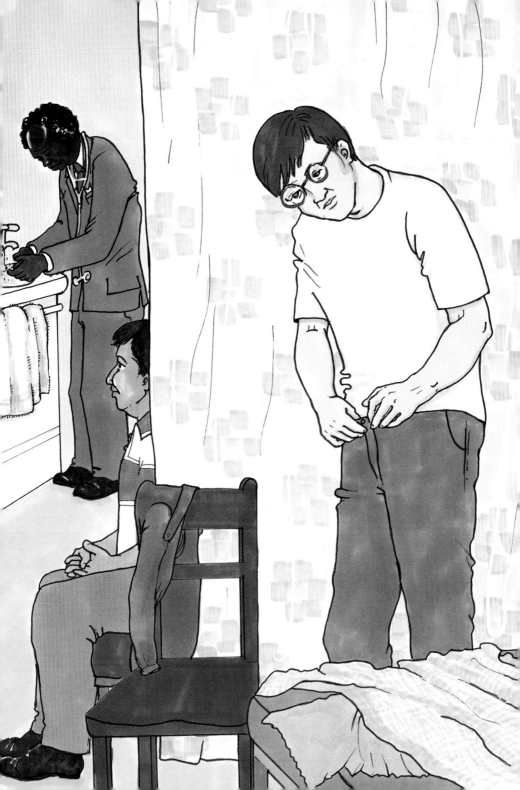

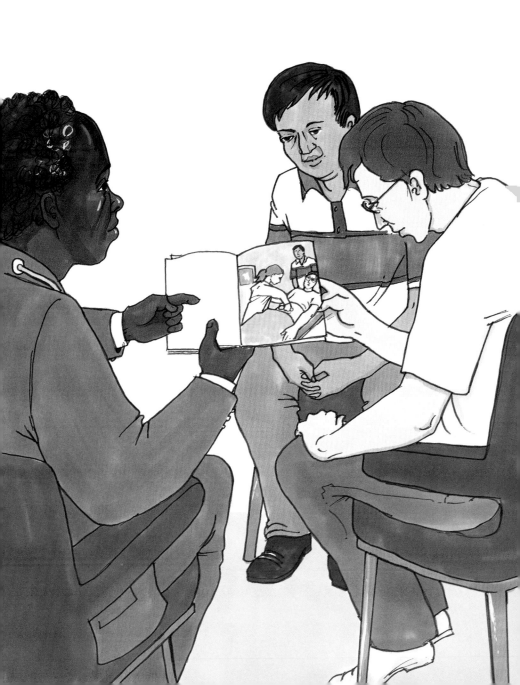

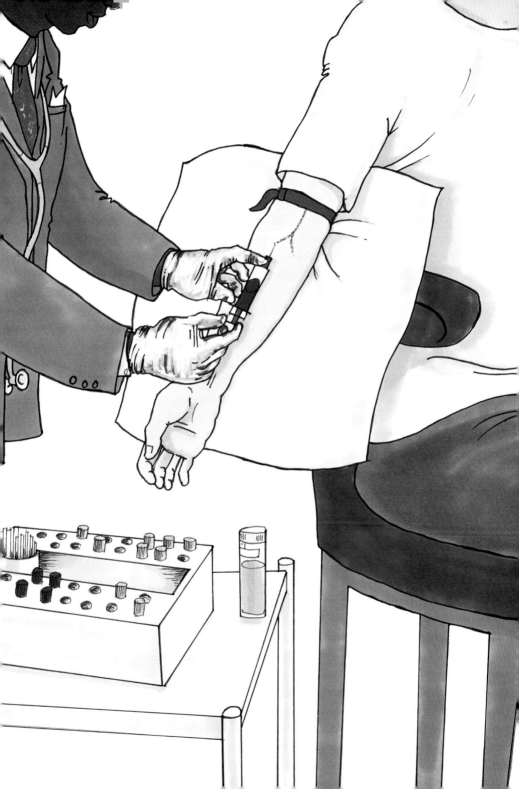

24

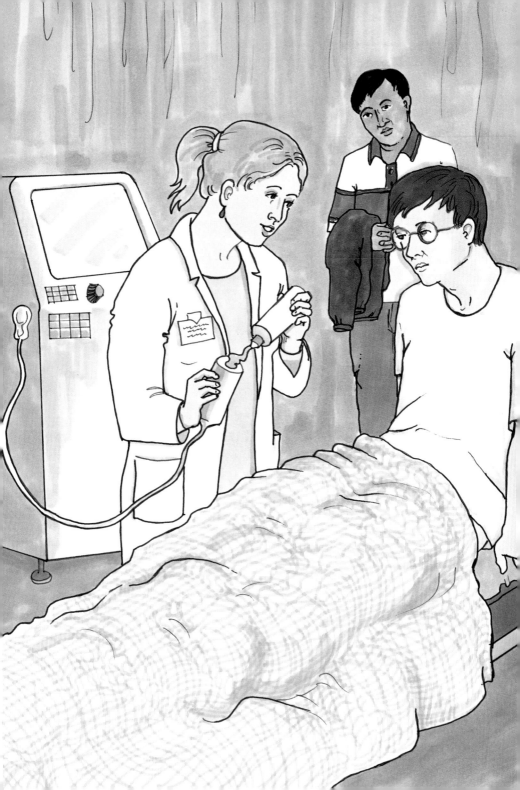

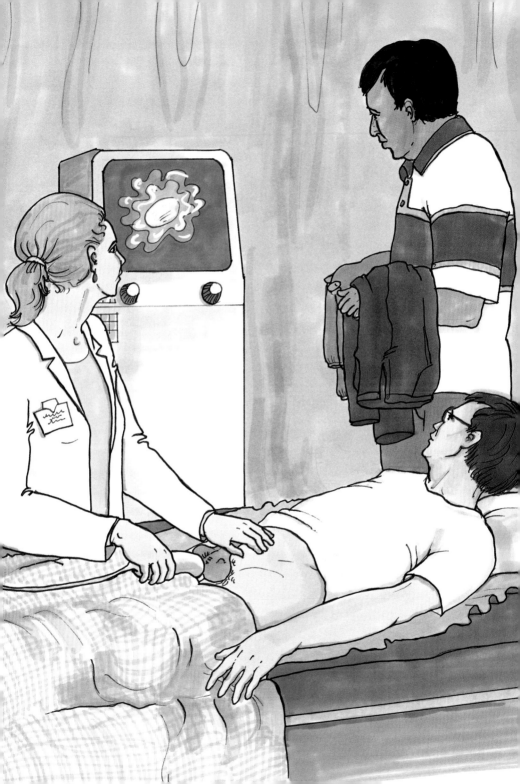

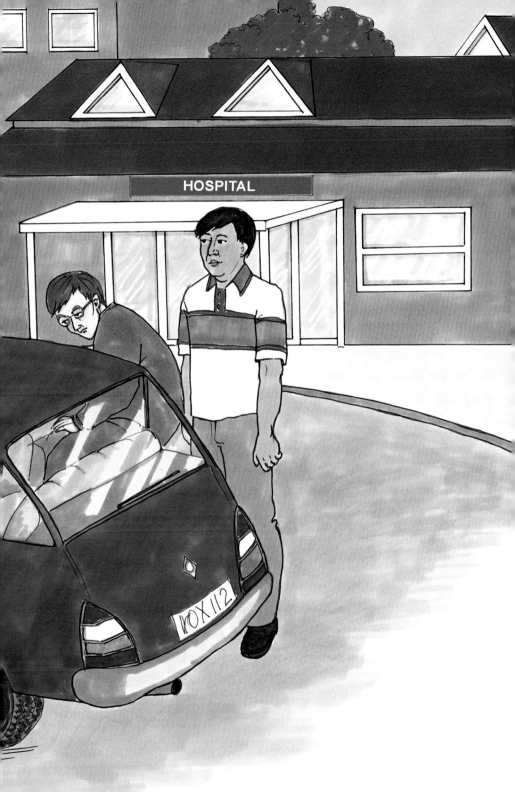

The following words are provided for people who want a ready-made story rather than tell their own.

1. Tom gets up.

2. Tom goes to the bathroom to take a shower.

3. Tom is having a shower.

4. He feels a lump in his ball (testicle).

5. He gets out of the shower and checks again. The lump is still there!

6. Tom phones his supporter Danny. He tells Danny about the lump.

7. Danny gets a book about 'looking after my balls'.

8. Tom gets dressed.

9a. Danny calls round and Tom lets him in. Danny brings the book with him.

9. Tom looks at the book with Danny.

10. The book shows what to look for, and how to check your balls.

11a. They visit the doctor as soon as possible.

11. They are in the waiting room of the doctor's surgery. Tom has the book.

12. Tom sees the doctor. He tells the doctor about the lump in his ball.

13. The doctor wants to check the lump. Tom thinks about it. He can say 'Yes, please check it', or 'No, thank you'.

14. Tom gets undressed. The doctor washes his hands.

15. The doctor feels Tom's tummy.

16. He checks Tom's balls and feels the lump.

17. The doctor finishes the examination. He washes his hands again. Tom gets dressed.

18. The doctor shows Tom what happens next. He wants Tom to have a scan.

19. Tom pees in a bottle so the doctor can test it.

20. The doctor takes a blood test from Tom's arm.

21a. Tom goes back home. He waves goodbye to Danny.

21. Tom relaxes with his cat Ralph and watches TV.

22. Tom gets a letter from the hospital. It asks him to go to the hospital for the scan.

23. He rings Danny and tells him about the letter.

24. Danny talks with Tom about what is going to happen at the hospital. They use the book again.

25. Tom thinks about it.

26a. He decides to have the scan. He goes to the hospital at the right time, with Danny.

26. They sit in the waiting room.

27. The hospital doctor is getting ready to take the scan.

28. Tom has the scan. The picture comes up on the screen.

29. Tom and Danny leave the hospital and get in the car.

30. Tom arrives home. Ralph the cat greets him.

31a. Some days later Tom returns to the doctor's with Danny.

31. The doctor tells Tom the result of the scan and the tests. It is good news. The lump is not cancer.

32. Tom goes back home. He is relieved. He gives Ralph a hug!

Looking after your balls (testicular awareness)

It is important for every man, with or without intellectual disabilities, to become familiar with his normal balls (testicles) and with normal changes in his balls. He should check them at convenient times in a private place, ideally during or after a shower or bath. Some people remember to check themselves at the beginning of every month. If a man notices an unusual change in his balls, such as a lump, swelling (one ball getting bigger) or pain and discomfort, he should make an appointment to see his doctor straight away. This is positive health awareness rather than a ritualised 'check for cancer'.

This book is particularly designed to help men with intellectual disabilities to learn more about their balls and about how to look after them. It is divided into two sections. The first tells the story of Tom, who finds a lump while checking his balls in the shower, seeks help straight away from his supporter and goes to see the GP. He has some further tests and an ultrasound scan and it is found that the lump is not due to cancer. The second part of the book gives guidance on looking after your balls and changes to look out for. This is called 'How to Look After My Balls'. This part of the book can be copied and used to provide leaflets illustrating testicular self-examination if required. You can also find this on our website: www.intellectualdisability.info under 'How to Look After My Balls'.

This book does not cover treatment for cancer, which is included in other books in the series, in particular *Getting On With Cancer*.

Testicular cancer

Cancer of the testicle is rare, but it is the most common type of cancer in young men (aged 20–39). Some people have a higher risk of developing the disease. If one or both of a boy's testicles have not descended by the age of seven he has a greater risk of developing testicular cancer later in life. The risk is higher if a close member of the family has been diagnosed with the disease. It is more common among men with Down's syndrome and with other genetic conditions. People with Down's syndrome are more likely to have testicles that have not descended into the scrotum. If someone using this book is unable to feel one or both of his testicles he should also tell his doctor about this, as ultrasound screening may be required.

Cancer can start as a small lump but it grows. It can move to other parts of the body. Testicular cancer is almost always curable if found early. The disease responds well to treatment even if it has spread to other parts of the body. More than nine out of ten patients are cured.

Symptoms

The early signs of testicular cancer are easy to spot. They include a hard lump on the front or side of a testicle. Swelling or enlargement of a testicle, an increase in firmness of a testicle, pain or discomfort in a testicle or in the scrotum and an unusual difference between one testicle and the other are also important changes. Other warning signs may include a heavy feeling in the scrotum and a dull ache in the lower stomach, groin or scrotum. The key signs, as illustrated in this book, are a lump, pain or discomfort and swelling.

Other problems

Not all problems mean that the person has cancer. For example, discomfort in his testicle (ball) might mean that he has an infection. Most lumps are benign, but it is important not to delay a visit to the doctor. Then the correct diagnosis can be made and the right treatment given.

Having a learning/intellectual disability

A person with an intellectual disability has a reduced ability to understand new or complex information, a difficulty in learning new skills and may be unable to cope independently. These difficulties started before adulthood and have a lasting effect on development.

Having an intellectual disability does not mean that the person will never understand the advice or treatment given. Some will not need this book to assist their understanding and will have good communication skills. A very few will find all information bewildering or will not have the comprehension to follow a sequence of pictures. Sometimes one or two carefully chosen pictures will be enough to explain what is required. Many people with intellectual disabilities need time and support to understand information, whether presented in simplified language or non-verbally.

Some medical words explained

Benign   A benign tumour is a lump, swelling or growth that is not cancer.

Blood test   The doctor may want to take some blood to see if it's OK. To do this the doctor will use a needle and some special bottles. The needle pricks your arm and the blood goes into the bottle. This does hurt a little bit and you may want to look away.

Cancer   Something growing in your body that shouldn't be there. It can grow and may move to other parts of your body. Some tumours are cancer, and some tumours are not cancer. 'Testicular cancer' or 'cancer of the testicle' starts in the testicle (ball).

Consent   The doctor must explain what kind of treatment or test they want to give you. They must explain what they want to do and why. They must explain what can happen if you don't have the treatment or test. Then you must decide if you want that treatment or test. Do you agree to it? Sometimes they ask you to write your name on a piece of paper, to say that you agree. If you don't agree, they cannot give you the treatment or test.

Examination   This is when the doctor has to do something to you to see how you are. For example, touching where you feel pain. You may have to take some clothes off. Then the doctor can see or feel properly.

Genetic abnormalities   Problems with genes. A gene is the unit through which likenesses and characteristics are passed from a parent to a child. Lots of genes together make up a chromosome.

Malignant   A malignant tumour is cancer. It will keep on growing bigger and bigger. It can also spread to other parts of the body.

Scrotum   The bag that contains the testicles (balls).

Supporter   Someone supporting the person with intellectual disabilities and helping with communication. This may be a family member, advocate or staff member.

Testicle   The testicles (balls) are located behind the penis in a pouch of skin called the scrotum. The testicles produce sperm and the hormone testosterone.

Testicular awareness   Getting to know your testicles (balls) so that you will notice any changes that are not normal.

Testicular self-examination (TSE)   Feeling your testicles to check for any changes, especially for lumps, swelling or discomfort. If you find anything unusual you can then seek help from a doctor.

Ultrasound scan   Shows on a screen what is under the skin. It uses sound waves that we cannot hear. The sound waves are harmless and do not hurt. They are also used in scans of babies before they are born.

Undescended testicle   One or both of your testicles have not descended into your scrotum. This means that you are unable to feel them. You should tell your GP, who might suggest an ultrasound scan to check that everything is OK.

Urine test   The doctor may ask you to go to the toilet and pee into a jug, a special bottle or a small pot. This is so that your pee (also called urine) can be tested. This can be a bit embarrassing.

Where to find help and advice in the UK

The Men's Health Forum (MHF)

Tavistock House
Tavistock Square
London WC1H 9HR

Tel: 020 7388 4449
Websites: www.menshealthforum.org.uk
www.malehealth.co.uk

The leading organisation in the UK promoting men's health through policy development, lobbying, research, professional training and awareness-raising. The MHF organises the annual National Men's Health Week in June and runs the UK's only independent, comprehensive men's health website in the UK.

The Orchid Cancer Appeal

St Bartholomew's Hospital
London EC1A 7BE

Tel: 020 7601 7808
Website: www.orchid-cancer.org.uk

Formed in 1996, the Orchid Cancer Appeal was the first registered charity dedicated to funding research into diagnosis, prevention and treatment of both testicular and prostate cancer as well as promoting awareness of these previously neglected diseases. The Orchid Cancer Appeal has produced a range of leaflets and other resource material free of charge to help people understand these cancers and their treatment.

Cancer Black Care
16 Dalston Lane
London E8 3AZ

Helpline: 020 7249 1097
Website: www.cancerblackcare.org

Offers information and advice, and addresses the cultural and emotional needs of Black and other minority ethnic people affected by cancer, as well as their families and friends.

Cancerbackup (now part of Macmillan Cancer Support)
89 Albert Embankment
London SE1 7UQ

Helpline: 0808 800 1234
Websites: www.cancerbackup.org.uk
www.macmillan.org.uk

Cancerbackup provides information and support to people with cancer, their families and friends. The Helpline is staffed by specialist cancer information nurses. The Macmillan website gives information on Macmillan services as well as other available cancer organisations and support agencies.

Services

Community teams for people with learning/ intellectual disabilities (CTPLDs). These are specialist multidisciplinary health and social care teams that support adults with intellectual disabilities and their families. Your GP or social services department should have the address of the local CTPLD.

Resource pack

Know Your Balls...Check 'Em Out. This educational resource pack aims to make young men aware of testicular cancer and the issues that surround it. The pack contains a 17-minute video aimed at 14- to 20-year-olds. Introduced by Chris Evans and Jonathan Ross, it is crammed full of celebrities, including some of Britain's top sportsmen. *Know Your Balls... Check 'Em Out* is designed to amuse while educating young men about testicular cancer. It takes a light-hearted and frank look at the serious subject of testicular cancer by (1) outlining possible symptoms, (2) showing what the treatment involves, (3) talking to patients, and (4) hearing from sportsmen who have experienced testicular cancer.

Supporting the video are: 100 information cards the size of credit cards, showing bullet-point essential information on one side and helpline numbers on the other; teacher's booklet; an A3 and an A4 poster and a pad of 100 quiz sheets. Total price £25.00 for the video resource pack and £28.00 for the DVD resource pack; price for the video alone £9.00 and for the DVD alone £12.00. Free of charge to schools, colleges, universities and non-profit-making organisations. Available from the Orchid Cancer Appeal, St Bartholomew's Hospital, London EC1A 7BE.

How to Look After My Balls

You can photocopy pages i to vii to use as a leaflet. You do not need to get special permission to do this and it is free of charge.

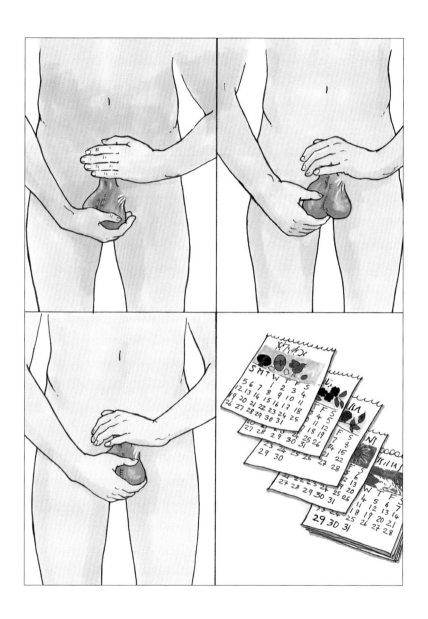

Check like this.

Check for:

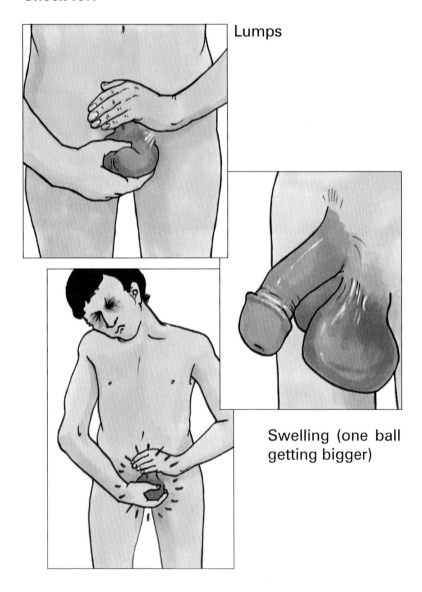

Lumps

Swelling (one ball getting bigger)

Pain or discomfort

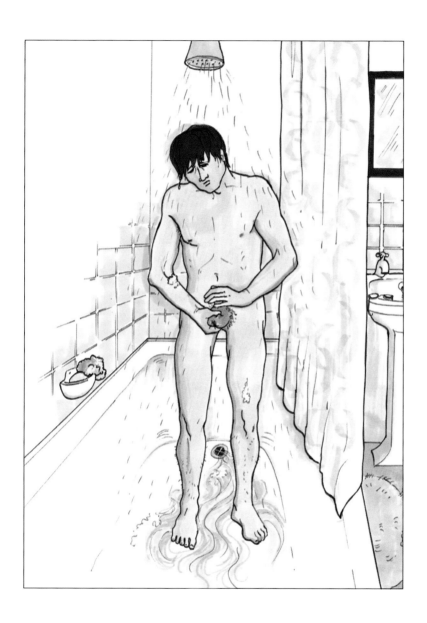

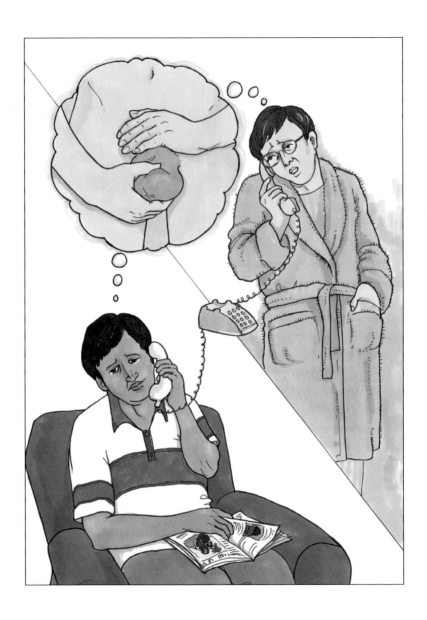

Ask for help straight away if you find something
wrong.

Don't wait.
Go and see your doctor.

Some other titles in the Books Beyond Words series

Using health services is explained in *Going to the Doctor*, *Going to Out-Patients* and *Going into Hospital*. *Getting On With Cancer* deals honestly with the unpleasant side of treatment but ends on a positive note. *Looking After My Breasts* and *Keeping Healthy 'Down Below'* are about breast and cervical screening.

Mugged tells what happens to a young man after he is attacked and robbed in the street. The book includes up-to-date advice about how to be a witness in court.

George Gets Smart is about personal cleanliness and shows how a man's life changes when he learns to keep clean and smart.

Three books cover access to criminal justice as a victim (witness) or as a defendant: *Supporting Victims*, *You're Under Arrest* and *You're On Trial*.

Food... Fun, Healthy and Safe demonstrates how choosing, cooking and eating food can be fun as well as healthy and safe. *Enjoying Sport and Exercise* encourages people to choose an activity and shows how to find out what is available to them locally.

Am I Going to Die? deals honestly and movingly with the physical and emotional aspects of dying. *When Somebody Dies* shows how bereavement counselling sessions and the support of friends help a man and a woman to feel less sad and cope with life better after someone they love dies. *When Dad Died* and *When Mum Died* take an honest and straightforward approach to death and grief in the family. The latest editions include guidelines and useful resources.

The books cost £10 each. To order copies or a leaflet giving more information about these books, please contact: Book Sales, Royal College of Psychiatrists, 17 Belgrave Square, London SW1X 8PG. Credit card orders can be taken by telephone (+44 (0)20 7235 2351, ext. 146). You can also order the books online at http://www.rcpsych.ac.uk/bbw